NEXT LEVEL
THINKING
Journal

Also by Joel Osteen

NEXT LEVEL THINKING
Journal

10 POWERFUL THOUGHTS
FOR A SUCCESSFUL
AND ABUNDANT LIFE

#1 *NEW YORK TIMES* BESTSELLING AUTHOR

JOEL OSTEEN

Faith Words

New York • Nashville

FaithWords
Hachette Book Group
1290 Avenue of the Americas
New York, NY 10104
faithwords.com
twitter.com/faithwords

First Edition: March 2019

FaithWords is a division of Hachette Book Group, Inc.
The FaithWords name and logo are trademarks of Hachette Book Group, Inc.

The publisher is not responsible for websites (or their content) that are not owned by the publisher.

The Hachette Speakers Bureau provides a wide range of authors for speaking events. To find out more, go to www.hachettespeakersbureau.com or call (866) 376-6591.

Literary development: Lance Wubbels Literary Services, Bloomington, Minnesota.

ISBN: 978-1-5460-2651-8

Printed in the United States of America

10 9 8 7 6 5 4 3 2 1

Contents

Introduction

We can all find reasons to live negative, bitter, as though we're at a disadvantage. Perhaps we came down with an illness, or somebody walked out of a relationship with us, or our boss overlooked us. Too often we focus on our past, our mistakes, our failures, limitations of how we grew up and what people think of us. It's easy to get discouraged, give up on our dreams, and just settle.

That is why I wrote my book *Next Level Thinking*. God created us to be free from all the shame, the guilt, the condemnation, the addictions, the feelings of never being good enough, and the carrying of pain of past hurts. It's interesting that before Jesus took His final breath on the cross, He declared, "It is finished." More than just declaring that His assignment on earth was finished, Jesus was stating in no uncertain terms that everything His assignment pertained to was finished—that He had provided us with everything we need to become everything He created us to be. It's done. Paid for. Finished!

This journal companion offers a practical tool that will help you harness insights from *Next Level Thinking* and help you see that everything you need to live a successful and abundant life has already been provided. All you have to do is believe it, receive it, and walk in it. It offers the same encouragement in daily doses supplemented by inspirational and thought-provoking material. You will find a wealth of scriptures, inspirational quotations, selected stories, prayers, and points for contemplation. The thoughts and questions addressed in the following pages will help you train yourself to leave behind the negative mind-sets, the scarcity mentality, and the limitations others have put on you.

In this journal, you'll learn ten powerful keys:

- Be a Barrier Breaker
- You Are Fully Loaded
- The Odds Are for You
- Move Up to the Next Level
- Recognize Your Value
- Live with the Boldness of a Son
- Know You Are Loved
- Approve Yourself
- Get the Contaminants Out
- Remove the Shame

This journal is an open door to self-discovery, so step through and begin the journey toward living the life you were born to live. Take the time to reflect on your life. Let the scriptures speak to your heart. If you are facing challenges or barriers, there are prayers and inspirational quotes to help remind you that God is with you each and every moment. Be still and listen to what God is saying through these words, then put words to your responses.

This is a journal to record life lessons that you don't want to forget. Underline important ideas within these pages, write yourself notes of encouragement in the margins as you read, and jot down fresh ideas that come to you as you read. Especially seek God's help and guidance regarding areas in which He may want to change you. What you record you remember. You will discover that it will bring clarity to what God has done, is doing, and wants to do in your life.

Journaling has also been shown to improve problem-solving abilities. Many people find that using a journal helps them to better assess their thoughts and feelings and to find clarity. The process of putting pen to paper and then seeing your words on the page can help you solve problems while keeping matters in perspective and priorities straight.

This journal is designed to provide you twenty days of daily inspiration and encouragement in your walk of faith. It is best to read day to day in a quiet place where you can meditate and contemplate for brief periods, away from the usual distractions.

Enjoy the process as you uncover the keys to help you learn to keep moving forward to the next levels of the good things God has in store.

NEXT LEVEL
THINKING

SECTION I

Be a Barrier Breaker

CHAPTER ONE

Take the Limitations Off

≫ *Key Truth* ≪

Instead of just fitting into your environment
and being like everyone else, why don't
you start seeing yourself as a barrier breaker?
You were created to excel. There is potential
in you right now just waiting to come out.
You have gifts that will cause new
doors to open, talent that will bring new
opportunities. Get rid of low expectations.
Break out of the mold.

S o often we let our environment, how we were raised, and other people's expectations of us set the limits for our life. We adapt to what's around us. It's so easy to just fit in, to go with the crowd, to be like everyone else. But God didn't create you to be average. He created you to go beyond the norm and leave your mark on this generation. You have seeds of greatness on the inside. You're supposed to go further than the people who raised you. You're supposed to live better, be more successful, and set a new standard.

Jesus speaks of how we are *in* the world, but we "are not *of* the world any more than [He is] *of* the world" (John 17:14). You may be *in* a limited environment, but you don't have to be *of* it. Don't let that environment get in you. If you see struggle, lack, and poverty long enough, your mind can become conditioned to thinking, *This is who I am. I'll always struggle. I'll never have enough.* No, that's where you are, that's not who you are. That may be what's been normal. The good news is, you're a barrier breaker. You have the power, the favor, the talent, and the ability to break out and go further. God breathed His life into you. He calls you the head and not the tail. Don't let your mind become conditioned for mediocrity. Don't let that change who you really are.

That's what happened to a friend of mine. He grew up in the projects, was very poor, and because of his poor home situation, he was labeled by the state as a "child at risk." From the time he was a little boy, that phrase become ingrained in his thinking: *There's no future for me. I'm a child at risk.* He just did what the rest of the crowd was doing. He adapted to his defeated, addicted environment. Believing he was at risk, he became at risk. His mind became conditioned with limitations, and his life followed his thoughts.

One day he got into trouble at school and was sent to the school counselor. She tried to reason with him, but he wouldn't listen. Finally he said to her, "Why are you even bothering with me? I've been told my whole life I'm a child at risk." She looked him in the eyes and said, "Listen to me: you are not a child at risk, you are a child at possibility." When he heard that, something ignited on the inside. He said to her, "What do you mean *at possibility?*" She said, "You are full of potential. You are smart, you are talented. There's so much you can become." That day a stronghold was broken in his thinking. He reconditioned his mind. Today, this man owns his own business and is very successful.

You have to get rid of the thoughts that are holding you back. You may not see how you can do it in your own ability, but you're not on your own. You have the most powerful force in the universe breathing in your direction. God created you to rise higher, to break barriers of the past, to overcome bad habits, and to be free from generational curses. God has already taken into account every detail of your life—every bad break, every negative comment, how you were raised, what somebody did or didn't do. He's factored that all into His plan. If you will stay in faith, instead of holding you back, it will propel you forward. Instead of defeating you, it will make you stronger. God knows how to take what was meant for your harm and use it to your advantage.

Consider This

Has anyone ever spoken truth like that into your life that broke a stronghold in your thinking? Or has a Scripture been used to break the power of thoughts that have held you back? Describe your experience and how God used that to change your life.

....

....

....

....

....

....

....

....

....

....

....

....

....

....

....

....

....

....

....

....

What the Scriptures Say

But Joseph said to [his brothers who had sold him into slavery], "Don't be afraid. Am I in the place of God? You intended to harm me, but God intended it for good to accomplish what is now being done, the saving of many lives."

Genesis 50:19–20

"Have I not commanded you? Be strong and courageous. Do not be afraid; do not be discouraged, for the LORD your God will be with you wherever you go."

Joshua 1:9

Thoughts for Today

Labels start out as little threads of self-dissatisfaction but ultimately weave together into a straightjacket of self-condemnation.

Lysa TerKeurst

I don't care what people call me, labels have the negative value of making smaller boundaries for people.

Michael Graves

God has great things in store for His people; they ought to have large expectations.

C. H. Spurgeon

....

....

....

....

....

....

....

....

....

....

....

....

....

....

A Prayer for Today

Father in heaven, thank You that no matter how people may have labeled me, You created me to rise higher, to break barriers of the past, to overcome bad habits, and to leave my mark upon this generation. Thank You that I am not limited by my education, by how I was raised, or by my environment, because You have put seeds of greatness in me and destined me to break out of a mold of mediocrity. I declare that mediocrity is finished and that with Your favor I will go to new levels where I could not go on my own. In Jesus' Name. Amen.

....
....
....
....
....
....
....
....
....
....
....
....
....
....
....
....
....

Takeaway Truth

You were created to excel. Somebody
may have labeled you "at risk," but the Creator
of the universe labels you "at possibility."
Dare to take some steps of faith. Life is flying by.
You don't have ten years to wait around. The odds
may be against you, but the Most High God is
for you. His favor on your life will cause you to go
to levels where you could not go on your own.
If you're going to be a barrier breaker,
you have to get rid of excuses.

CHAPTER TWO

Defy the Odds

›› *Key Truth* ‹‹

God is saying, "This is a new day. You're a barrier breaker. I'm going to take you further than you've imagined. I'm going to help you set a new standard. You're going to defy the odds." Now do your part. Let this seed take root in your spirit. Don't talk yourself out of it. Get in agreement with God. You and God are a majority.

For years, experts said that no one would ever be able to run a mile in under four minutes. They studied the human body and thought it would collapse under that much pressure. Scientists said it was not only dangerous to try, but it was literally impossible. But a young man named Roger Bannister didn't believe the negative reports. He didn't let his mind become conditioned to thinking it couldn't be done. In May 1954, he made history by running a mile in under four minutes. What's interesting is that forty-six days later, someone else broke the four-minute mile. Within ten years, 336 people had run the mile in under four minutes' time. It hadn't happened in all the previous years of track and field history, now it was happening all the time. Why was that? The barrier was broken in people's minds. For years runners had believed what the experts said. Once that barrier was removed, they were able to do things that seemed impossible. Has your mind become conditioned to thinking you can't accomplish your dreams, you can't get well, you'll never break that addiction? If you'll do as Roger did and recondition your mind, start thinking better, believing that you're a can-do person, knowing that you have seeds of greatness, you too will break barriers that you thought were impossible.

And here's the beauty: when you break a barrier, you make it easier for those who come after you. You're paving the way for your children, for your relatives. That's what it means to set a new standard. That's what a young man in the Scripture named Hezekiah did. He was raised in a very dysfunctional home. His father was King Ahaz of Judah, who set up idols for the people to worship. He was a very hard king and cruel to the people. Because he didn't honor God, the nation went downhill and became very poor. Five different armies came against Judah, and Judah lost every battle. The nation was decimated. You would think that Ahaz would have learned his lesson, turned to God, asked for His help, but it was just the opposite. He closed the doors of the temple and began to sell off sacred treasures. Hezekiah was raised in this environment of compromise, defeat, and mediocrity. He could have turned out like his dad; he could have adapted to that environment. But Hezekiah understood this principle. When he became king, the first thing Hezekiah did, before repairing the roads or getting the economy going, was to reopen the temple. He turned the nation back toward God.

His father chose to compromise and to push people down, but Hezekiah's attitude was, *I might have been born into mediocrity, but I'm not settling here. I'm going to put an end to this generational curse, and I'm going to start a generational blessing. Mediocrity is finished.* Hezekiah was a barrier breaker. You may be in some kind of limited environment. If Hezekiah were here today, he would tell you, "You don't have to stay there." How you start is not important. How you finish is what matters. Do yourself and your family a favor. Break out of that mold. Don't pass negative things down to the next generation. You can be the difference maker. You can be the one who sets your family on a course to honoring God, a course of blessing, favor, and victory.

Consider This

Glenn Cunningham went from being a boy who was told that he would never walk again to breaking the world record in the mile run in 1934. That required an amazing determination to overcome all the odds through a spirit of faith. Search out and write down Scriptures that speak to the areas where you need to break barriers as Cunningham did.

....

....

....

....

....

....

....

....

....

....

....

....

....

....

....

....

....

What the Scriptures Say

Now to him who is able to do immeasurably more than all we ask or imagine, according to his power that is at work within us...

Ephesians 3:20

You, dear children, are from God and have overcome them, because the one who is in you is greater than the one who is in the world.

1 John 4:4

....
....
....
....
....
....
....
....
....
....
....
....
....
....
....
....
....
....

Thoughts for Today

There are no constraints on the human mind, no walls around the human spirit, no barriers to our progress except those we ourselves erect.

Ronald Reagan

Alleged "impossibilities" are opportunities for our capacities to be stretched.

Charles Swindoll

Don't assume you have to be extraordinary to be used by God. You don't have to have exceptional gifts, talents, abilities, or connections. God specializes in using ordinary people whose limitations and weaknesses make them ideal showcases for His greatness and glory.

Nancy Leigh DeMoss

....
....
....
....
....
....
....
....
....
....
....
....
....

A Prayer for Today

Father in heaven, thank You that I can quit thinking about what I didn't get, what I can't do, how the odds are against me, because You and I are a majority. Thank You that You have given me everything I need in Christ to defy the odds and break through the barriers that are trying to hold me back. I refuse to let my environment and what people have said about me to set limits of mediocrity for my life. I believe that You are breathing on my life and that You'll help me defy the odds and accomplish my dreams. In Jesus' Name. Amen.

....

....

....

....

....

....

....

....

....

....

....

....

....

....

....

....

Takeaway Truth

Recondition your mind. Get rid of
strongholds that are keeping you back.
Stir up your seeds of greatness. Defy the odds.
Be a barrier breaker. If you do this, I believe
and declare God is going to breathe on your
life in a new way. You're going to go beyond
barriers of the past, overcome obstacles,
and accomplish dreams. You're
going to become everything God
created you to be.

NEXT LEVEL
THINKING

You Are Fully Loaded

CHAPTER THREE

Nobody Can Beat You at Being You

» *Key Truth* «

When God created you, He put in you everything
you need to fulfill your destiny. He gave you
the talent you need, the creativity, the strength.
You're the right size, and you have the right
looks, the right personality, and the right family.
You are fully loaded and completely equipped
for the race that's been designed for you.

When God created you, He didn't just create you and say, "Let's see what he can do." God is precise. He's intentional, down to the smallest detail, and when He laid out the plan for your life, He studied it carefully. He thought about what you would need, and what it would take to get you there, then He matched you with your world. He gave you the talent you need, the creativity, the strength. You're the right size, and you have the right looks, the right personality, and the right family. You didn't get shortchanged. You are fully loaded and completely equipped for the race that's been designed for you.

Now quit wishing you were something different: "If I had a better personality, I could do something great." "If I came from a different family..." "If I weren't so small..." Have a new perspective. If you needed to be taller, God would've made you taller. If you needed a different personality, He would've given you one. If you needed to be another nationality, you would be another nationality. God doesn't make mistakes. You're not faulty. You have been fearfully and wonderfully made.

When God created the mountains, oceans, sunsets, animals, and butterflies, He said, "That was good." But when God created you, when He saw how magnificent you are, how strong, how attractive, and how talented you are, He said, "That was *very* good." In Ephesians, He calls you "a masterpiece." When the Creator of the universe says, "You are very good," that means you are just right! Now don't go around feeling shortchanged, as though somehow you're lacking, you didn't get enough, you can't do what others can do. Quit comparing yourself to others and run your race. Be who God created you to be. You are an original. You have something to offer the world that nobody else has. Let your gifts shine. Show your talent, your personality, your style. We don't need an imitation. We don't need a copy. We need the original you.

When you want what somebody else has, when you wish you had their looks, their talent, their personality, the truth is, if you had it, it wouldn't be a blessing. It would be a burden. It wasn't designed for you. The reason it works for them is because it fits them. They're walking in their anointing. You are not anointed to be somebody else. As long as you're trying to be like them, you'll be frustrated. The anointing on your life is to be who God called you to be. Be confident in what you have. Next level thinking says you have the right looks, the right talent, and the right personality.

I've learned that it's easy to be me. I don't have to pretend or perform. That takes all the pressure off. I can relax and just be myself. When you're comfortable with who you are, when you're not trying to impress people or to be something that you're not, your own uniqueness will come out. Your talent will come out in greater ways. The right people will show up. Why? Because you've stepped into the anointing on your life. Be you. You are powerful when you're you.

Consider This

Too often when we see someone who's more talented, more successful, more blessed, there's a tendency to be envious. If we're not careful, before long we'll be competing with them, trying to outperform them, outdress them, outdrive them, outwork them. What is the problem when you start to compete with others?

....
....
....
....
....
....
....
....
....
....
....
....
....
....
....
....
....
....

What the Scriptures Say

So God created human beings in his own image. In the image of God he created them; male and female he created them.

Genesis 1:27 NLT

"[David], if that had not been enough, I would have given you much, much more."

2 Samuel 12:8 NLT

....
....
....
....
....
....
....
....
....
....
....
....
....
....
....
....
....
....

Thoughts for Today

People travel to wonder at the height of the mountains, at the huge waves of the seas, at the long course of the rivers, at the vast compass of the ocean, at the circular motion of the stars, and yet they pass by themselves without wondering.

Augustine

You are the result of the attentive, careful, thoughtful, intimate, detailed, creative work of God. Your personality, your sex, your height, and your features are what they are because God made them precisely that way. He made you the way He did because that is the way He wants you to be.

James Hufstetler

You say, "If I had a little more, I should be very satisfied." You make a mistake. If you are not content with what you have, you would not be satisfied if it were doubled.

Charles Spurgeon

A Prayer for Today

Father in heaven, thank You that I didn't accidentally get my personality, my looks, my gifts, my skin color, or my height. Thank You that I am Your masterpiece and fearfully and wonderfully made, and that You have declared me to be very good. Help me be content to be who You created me to be and to stop comparing myself to others. I believe that I am fully loaded for the race that You designed for me and that You will help me be the best that I can be. In Jesus' Name. Amen.

....
....
....
....
....
....
....
....
....
....
....
....
....
....
....
....
....

Takeaway Truth

Nobody can beat you at being you.
You can be a better you than anybody in
the world. You have an advantage. You've been
anointed to be you. When you're who you are,
you can be quiet and be powerful. You can
be small and be powerful. You can be behind
the scenes and be powerful. The whole key
is to be you, because when you're you,
there's a favor, a blessing, a grace that
is unique to your life.

CHAPTER FOUR

Know Who You Are and Who You're Not

» *Key Truth* «

If you don't know who you are, you can spend your life trying to be something that you're not. Knowing what you're not will help you stay focused on becoming who you are, because there will always be pressures to be this, to be that, to be the other. You can't let outside pressures and other people squeeze you into becoming something that you're not.

n the Scripture, John the Baptist was baptizing people and gaining a lot of attention. At one point the Jewish leaders came and asked him if he was the Christ. Without missing a beat John said, "I am not the Messiah" (John 1:20). It's important to know not only who you are, but to know who you're not. If you don't know this, you can spend your life trying to be something that you're not. John had no problem saying, "I am not the Messiah." He was saying, "I don't have to be the Messiah to feel good about myself. I'm content with who God made me to be."

If you're trying to be something you're not, you'll be frustrated. There's no grace for it. It will be a constant struggle, always like it's uphill. In the Scripture, King Saul lost the throne when he saw David rising higher and gaining more influence than him. Instead of celebrating David, he became jealous. When people started singing, "Saul has slain his thousands," he was happy (1 Sam. 29:5). But when the song continued, "And David his tens of thousands," Saul's whole perspective changed. He was no longer content with his success. Now he was envious. He basically spent the rest of his life trying to be David. All he had to do was realize: "I am not David. God has blessed him in a different way."

We have to understand the sovereignty of God. It might not seem fair to us, and it doesn't always make sense to us, but God's ways are not our ways. The Scripture talks about how God has given to every person different gifts, different talents, according to our own ability. Everyone doesn't get the same, but what He gave you is what you need to fulfill your destiny. Whether you're a Saul and you can defeat a thousand, or you're a David and you can defeat ten thousand, the right attitude is, *I'm going to take what God's given me and make the most of it.* Don't compete, don't compare, just run your race.

When I first started ministering, I was young and didn't have much experience, and I had a lot of people giving me their opinions. They told me how to lead the church, how to minister, what I should speak on. And sometimes it wasn't what they said, it was what they implied. I could feel the pressure to be who they wanted me to be. They were good people, but people didn't breathe life into you. People didn't lay out your plan and purpose. People didn't put gifts and talents on the inside. I was always respectful, but I was firm. When I heard a lot of their advice, I knew it wasn't what God had put in my heart, and I had to be bold and say, "I am not that. This is who I am."

It takes a mature person to recognize what you're not. Knowing what you're not will help you stay focused on becoming who you are, because there will always be pressures to be this, to be that, to be the other. Everyone will have opinions about you, but down in your heart you know who you are. You can't let the outside pressures and other people squeeze you into becoming something that you're not. You have to be strong. It's your destiny. People may mean well, they may love you, but if it doesn't bear witness in your spirit, you have to be bold and say, like John the Baptist, "That is not who I am."

Consider This

Who do you feel others think you are, and how have they put pressure on you to become what they think you should be? Who do you think you are, and who do you know that you are not? What is God showing you about the person He wants you to be?

....
....
....
....
....
....
....
....
....
....
....
....
....
....
....
....
....
....
....

What the Scriptures Say

"His word is in my heart like a fire, a fire shut up in my bones.
I am weary of holding it in; indeed, I cannot."

Jeremiah 20:9

"I will bless her and will surely give you a son by her.
I will bless her so that she will be the mother of nations;
kings of peoples will come from her."

Genesis 17:16

....
....
....
....
....
....
....
....
....
....
....
....
....
....
....
....
....

Thoughts for Today

Learn to say no to the good so you can say yes to the best.

John Maxwell

When you care more about what others think of you than what God knows about you, you've lost perspective on what really matters.

Christine Caine

God is busy making you someone no one else has ever been.

Beth Moore

....

....

....

....

....

....

....

....

....

....

....

....

....

....

....

....

A Prayer for Today

Father in heaven, thank You that the gifts and the talents and all that You've put into me are all that I need to fulfill my destiny. Thank You that I can take what You've given me and make the very most of it, not competing or comparing with others, but just running my race. Help me to know both who I am and who I am not so I can be strong and develop the gifts that You have given. I believe and declare that what has been shut up in my spirit is going to be released and that You will take me to the next level. In Jesus' Name. Amen.

....

....

....

....

....

....

....

....

....

....

....

....

....

....

....

....

....

Takeaway Truth

God has put greatness in you.
He's given you gifts, creativity, and dreams.
He created you to leave your mark on
this generation. There is something significant
about you, something that will cause you
to stand out. What's been shut up in your
spirit is about to be released. It's going to be
bigger, more rewarding, more fulfilling than
you ever imagined. Stir up those gifts.
Stir up that faith.

NEXT LEVEL
THINKING

The Odds Are for You

CHAPTER FIVE

Don't Let the Odds Fool You

» *Key Truth* «

The odds may be against you, but the Most High God is for you, and He is a supernatural God. He parts Red Seas. He turns water into wine. He opens the eyes of the blind. Your circumstances may look impossible, but the God Who can do the impossible is working behind the scenes arranging things in your favor, turning negative situations around.

t's easy to go through life thinking of all the reasons why we can't be successful, why we won't get well, or why we'll never meet the right person. We look at our situations in the natural and think the odds are against us. But as long as you think the odds are against you, you will get stuck where you are. You have the most powerful force in the universe breathing in your direction. God has crowned you with favor. He has armed you with strength for every battle. He wouldn't have allowed that difficulty if He wasn't going to turn it around and use it to your advantage. The odds may be against you, but since the Most High God is for you, that means the odds are for you.

This is what happened to a man in the Scripture named Gideon. The Midianites and two other armies came against him. They were about to attack the Israelites. Gideon sent word to his men to come and fight. Thirty-two thousand warriors showed up, but the enemy forces had one hundred and thirty-five thousand men. I can imagine Gideon was discouraged. He was outnumbered five to one, when God said to him, "You have too many men. If you defeat the Midianites, you will think you did it in your own strength." He instructed Gideon to let everyone who was afraid go home, and twenty-two thousand men left. Gideon nearly passed out. Two-thirds of his army went home. He didn't like these odds anymore. When he thought it couldn't get any worse, God said, "Gideon, you still have too many." He told him to eliminate even more men, and Gideon was finally left with only three hundred men to fight an army of over one hundred thousand. These odds seemed impossible. It looked as though Gideon would be wiped out. But what Gideon didn't realize was that God wasn't setting him back, He was setting him up. He was about to show out in Gideon's life.

Gideon and those three hundred men went to the enemy's camp in the middle of the night, blew their trumpets and let out a loud shout. The Midianites got confused in the darkness and began to fight among themselves. The Israelites defeated them, and they hardly had to lift a finger to do it. It had looked like a setback, but the truth was that God was setting Gideon up. He was putting him in position to show Himself strong.

When the odds seem like they're against you, and the obstacles look bigger, stronger, and more powerful, don't worry. As with Gideon, it is a setup. God is about to make things happen that you could never make happen. He is going to turn that situation around without you having to go to battle. He is going to heal you without the extensive treatment. He is going to promote you without all of the qualifications.

Keep the right perspective. Next level thinking says the odds are for you. You may feel like the underdog, but you and God are a majority. You don't need everyone to be for you. You don't have to have all the support and encouragement. You have the One Who matters. The Most High God is breathing in your direction. God wants to give you victory to where people know the Lord is on your side.

Consider This

Read the story in Daniel 3 of the three Hebrew teenagers, Shadrach, Meshach, and Abednego, who wouldn't bow down to the king's golden idol. Describe a situation in your past or present where the odds against you looked or look impossible. What is the right perspective to take when you feel like the underdog?

What the Scriptures Say

"And I will harden Pharaoh's heart, and he will pursue them. But I will gain glory for myself through Pharaoh and all his army, and the Egyptians will know that I am the LORD."

Exodus 14:4

I can do all things [which He has called me to do] through Him who strengthens and empowers me [to fulfill His purpose— I am self-sufficient in Christ's sufficiency; I am ready for anything and equal to anything through Him who infuses me with inner strength and confident peace.]

Philippians 4:13 AMP

....
....
....
....
....
....
....
....
....
....
....
....
....
....

Thoughts for Today

Abraham's unwavering faith arose from his great thoughts of Him Who had promised. He kept saying to himself, He is able, He is able. He knew that God would not have said what He could not perform. He knew that the God of nature was Lord of the nature He had made. He knew that no word of the Almighty was destitute of power. He fed his faith by cherishing lofty and profound thoughts of God's infinite resources. There rang in his heart the assurance, I am El Shaddai.

F. B. Meyer

What does a child do whose mother or father allows something to be done that it cannot understand? There is only one way to peace. The loving child trusts.

Amy Carmichael

We cannot always trace God's hand, but we can always trust God's heart.

Charles Spurgeon

....
....
....
....
....
....
....
....
....
....

A Prayer for Today

Father in heaven, thank You that when the odds seem like they're most against me, when the obstacles look bigger, stronger, and more powerful than anything I can handle, You are about to make things happen that I could never make happen. Thank You that You're bigger than any sickness, greater than any addiction, and more powerful than any opponent. I believe that if I stay in faith, You will give me victory to where others will see and know that You are on my side. In Jesus' Name. Amen.

....
....
....
....
....
....
....
....
....
....
....
....
....
....
....
....
....

Takeaway Truth

Don't let the odds fool you. Don't let the fact that you don't see a way cause you to think it wasn't meant to be. No, get ready. This is a setup. This is not the time to give up. This is the time to stir your faith up. God is about to show out. He is about to make you a testimony. He is going to do something that people cannot deny. They are going to know the Lord is on your side.

CHAPTER SIX

The Odds Cannot Stop You

» *Key Truth* «

God spoke worlds into creation. He didn't google it to see if it was possible. He didn't try to figure out a way. He is the way. He doesn't check with the odds to see if you can reach your destiny. He speaks and it becomes your destiny. God is not limited by your background. He is all-powerful. He can take nothing and make something magnificent.

n the Scripture, Mary and Martha sent word to their friend Jesus that their brother, Lazarus, was very sick. Jesus was in a different city, and they thought that He would come right away and pray for Lazarus. They knew that He could heal their brother. One day passed, and Jesus didn't show up. I am sure that Martha thought, *Jesus, where are You? What's taking You so long?* Another day went by, but still no sign of Jesus. Finally Lazarus died. When Jesus arrived at their house, Lazarus had been in the tomb for four days. Mary and Martha were so upset. They said, "Jesus, if You had been here, our brother would still be alive." The odds weren't that good when he was sick, but now that he was dead, they looked impossible. Lazarus was already wrapped up like a mummy in grave clothes. Against all apparent odds, Jesus went to the tomb, spoke to Lazarus and told him to come back to life, and Lazarus did! It was a great miracle.

Sometimes God will wait on purpose until the odds are way against you. You're ready to bury the dream, bury the promise, bury the relationship. You don't see a way it can work out. But God's ways are not our ways. Mary and Martha were praying for a healing, but God had something better in store. He had a resurrection. What you're tempted to give up on, you don't see how it can happen, maybe God is not going to do it the way you're thinking. Maybe He has something better for you.

We tried twice to buy property on which to build a new sanctuary. Both times the properties were sold out from under us. We couldn't find any more large tracts of land. I was discouraged. I didn't think we would ever have a bigger sanctuary. Then one day the Compaq Center suddenly became available. I was praying for a healing, but God had a resurrection, something better than I had ever dreamed.

The odds may be totally against you today, but can I tell you that God is totally for you? He has not brought you this far to leave you. Your circumstances may look dead. You've been asking and asking, but God didn't show up on time. Dare to trust Him. He has you in the palms of His hands. You may not see anything happening, but He is working behind the scenes, and when He speaks, dead things come back to life. God controls the universe. The odds do not determine what He can and cannot do.

What's interesting is that most of the Jewish people who were very against Jesus believed that the spirit left the body three days after a person died. It wasn't a coincidence that Jesus waited until the fourth day to show up. He did this on purpose, so when He raised Lazarus, there wouldn't be any doubt about it. I love the fact that from that moment forward Lazarus became a living testimony. Lazarus defied the odds. Sometimes God will let the odds become greater so not just you, but also your critics, your neighbors, your relatives, and your coworkers won't be able to deny what God has done. That's what God wants to do for you, to show you His favor in such a way that people notice, that you stand out. You're going to become a living testimony.

Consider This

In the book of Genesis, it talks about how God created the heavens and the earth out of nothing. He started the universe with odds of zero. What does that show that He can do for you?

....

....

....

....

....

....

....

....

....

....

....

....

....

....

....

....

....

....

....

....

What the Scriptures Say

"For my thoughts are not your thoughts, neither are your ways my ways," declares the Lord. "As the heavens are higher than the earth, so are my ways higher than your ways and my thoughts than your thoughts."

Isaiah 55:8–9

Trust God from the bottom of your heart; don't try to figure out everything on your own. Listen for God's voice in everything you do, everywhere you go; he's the one who will keep you on track.

Proverbs 3:5–6 MSG

Thoughts for Today

The life of faith is not a life of mounting up with wings, but a life of walking and not fainting. Faith never knows where it is being led, but it loves and knows the One who is leading.

Oswald Chambers

Faith does not operate in the realm of the possible. There is no glory for God in that which is humanly possible. Faith begins where man's power ends.

George Müller

Never be afraid to trust an unknown future to a known God.

Corrie ten Boom

....

....

....

....

....

....

....

....

....

....

....

....

....

....

A Prayer for Today

Father in heaven, thank You that You are the amazing God Who spoke worlds into creation out of nothing and Who brings dead things back to life. Thank You that Your ways are so far greater than our ways and that You can give us resurrections when we're asking for healings. When circumstances and people come against me, help me to remember that the odd are for me. I dare to trust You and to believe that You have something better for me than I have ever dreamed. In Jesus' Name. Amen.

....
....
....
....
....
....
....
....
....
....
....
....
....
....
....
....

Takeaway Truth

You are God's prized possession. He breathed His life into you. You have the DNA of Almighty God. There may be odds against you in certain areas, but they cannot stop you. God has destined you to leave your mark. Don't let the odds discourage you. Don't let what you think is not going to happen talk you out of believing. Even if the odds are zero in a million, all God has to do is speak and the odds change in your favor.

NEXT LEVEL
THINKING

Move Up to the Next Level

CHAPTER SEVEN

This Is a New Day

» *Key Truth* «

When Jesus hung on the cross, before He took His final breath, He said, "It is finished." He wasn't just talking about His life and how He had finished His purpose. He was putting an end to all the negative things that could keep us from our destiny. He was saying, in effect, "The guilt, the low self-esteem, the mediocrity— it is all finished."

We all have things that are trying to hold us back, whether it's guilt from past mistakes, temptations that we can't seem to overcome, or a dysfunction that's been passed down to us. It's easy to learn to accept it and think that's who we are, but God didn't create you to go through life weighed down by addictions, dysfunction, guilt, or the past. He created you to be free.

Instead of accepting the addiction and thinking, *This is the way it's always going to be. Everybody in my family has it*, you need to announce to that addiction, "Jesus said, 'It is finished.' You don't control me. You can't keep me from my destiny. The price has been paid. I am free. I am clean. I am whole." As long as you accept the addiction, you're allowing it to stay. But when you tell the addiction, tell the past mistakes, tell the poverty, "It is finished. This is not who I am. I am blessed. I am prosperous. I am victorious," in the unseen realm, strongholds are broken, chains are loosed, and favor is released.

Are there things you're living with to which you need to say, "It is finished"? Are you going around feeling guilty, down on yourself because of past mistakes, not expecting anything good? You need to announce to that guilt, "It is finished. I'm done beating myself up, living condemned. God's mercy is bigger than my mistakes. I am redeemed. I am restored. I am forgiven, and I am excited about my future." Are you living with a sense of shame, feeling inferior because of how somebody treated you? Perhaps they did you wrong and walked away, and now the accuser whispers, "It's because you're not good enough. You're not attractive enough. You don't deserve to be loved." Announce to that shame, "It is finished. I'm not inferior or unworthy. I know who I am. I am a child of the Most High God. I'm wearing a crown of favor. I have royal blood flowing through my veins."

No matter what someone did or didn't do to you, it does not change who you are. You may have had bad breaks and gone through unfair situations, but don't have a victim mentality; have a victor mentality. God says He will pay you back double for the unfair things that have happened. That person who did you wrong and thought they were hurting you—the truth is, they were helping you. They qualified you for double. They thought they were setting you back, but in reality they were setting you up. Now, do your part and say to the self-pity, "It is finished. I'm not living discouraged, dwelling on my disappointments and reliving my hurts. I'm letting go of the old, and I'm moving up to the next level that God has in store. Father, thank You that double is coming my way."

The past, the hurts, the regrets—it is finished. The poverty, the lack, the limited mind-sets—it is finished. The addictions, the depression, the dysfunction, the guilt, the shame, the self-pity—it is finished. This is a new day. Things that have held you back are being broken right now. You're going to step into a new level of freedom. You're going to break generational curses and start generational blessings. You're about to see beauty for ashes, healing, promotion, and breakthroughs. It's headed your way!

Consider This

In John 5, the man who had been disabled for thirty-eight years shows us that as long as we're making excuses for where we are, we're going to get stuck. What are some of the excuses you have made or are making for where you are? What truth about God will enable you to get rid of the excuses?

What the Scriptures Say

When he had received the drink, Jesus said, "It is finished."
With that, he bowed his head and gave up his spirit.

John 19:30

Instead of your [former] shame you shall have a twofold
recompense; instead of dishonor and reproach [your people]…
shall possess double [what they had forfeited];
everlasting joy shall be theirs.

Isaiah 61:7 AMPC

....
....
....
....
....
....
....
....
....
....
....
....
....
....
....
....
....

Thoughts for Today

Our yesterdays present irreparable things to us; it is true that we have lost opportunities that will never return, but God can transform this destructive anxiety into a constructive thoughtfulness for the future. Let the past sleep, but let it sleep on the bosom of Christ. Leave the Irreparable Past in His hands, and step out into the Irresistible Future with Him.

Oswald Chambers

We cannot change our past. We cannot change the fact that people act in a certain way. We cannot change the inevitable. The only thing we can do is play on the one string we have, and that is our attitude.

Charles Swindoll

Faith sees the invisible, believes the unbelievable, and receives the impossible.

Corrie ten Boom

....

....

....

....

....

....

....

....

....

....

....

....

A Prayer for Today

Father, thank You that when Jesus hung on the cross and said,
"It is finished," He put an end to all the negative things that
could keep me from my destiny. Thank You that the price has
been paid and that the chains of guilt, condemnation, struggle,
inferiority, shame, insecurity, and mediocrity have been broken.
I am redeemed, restored, forgiven, and blessed to be Your
child with royal blood flowing in my veins. I'm letting go
of the old and getting ready for the double that is
coming my way. In Jesus' Name. Amen.

Takeaway Truth

We all can find a reason to live negatively, thinking we're at a disadvantage. I'm asking you to get rid of the excuses. It's time to say, "It is finished. I'm done thinking about what I didn't get, what didn't work out, who hurt me." You have to tell the past, tell the self-pity, tell the discouragement, "It is finished." As long as you justify your condition, you're giving it permission to stay.

CHAPTER EIGHT

Set a New Standard

» Key Truth «

You may have been raised in a limited environment. You can set a new standard. Where you start is not important. Where you finish is what matters. God is going to use you to start a generational blessing. Where you come from is not who you are. You are blessed, you are free, you are talented, and you are a child of the Most High God.

We all could come up with excuses to settle where we are. It's time to announce to anything that's holding you back, "It is finished. This is a new day. I'm drawing the line in the sand. As for me and my house, we will serve the Lord. We will accomplish our dreams and become everything we were created to be."

You may have to separate yourself from people who see you only for who you used to be and not for who you're about to become. Some people who knew you back then will try to keep you in the same box that you grew up in. They'll try to put limitations on you: "You can't accomplish that dream. You're not that talented. You'd better play it safe."

In the Scripture, this is what happened with David. His family didn't see him as a giant killer or as a king. They discounted him. David's father, Jesse, didn't even bother to bring him in from the shepherds' field when the prophet Samuel was choosing one of his eight sons as the next king of Israel. Jesse thought, *Ah, it's just David. He's so small and so young. He doesn't have the experience.* But people don't determine your destiny. What they say about you and how they try to make you feel cannot stop what God has ordained for your life. You need to distance yourself from people who are always trying to put limitations on you and talk you out of what God has put in your heart. Sometimes that includes the people who have known you the longest, because they can see you only one way.

Jesus' own brothers did not believe in Him until after He rose from the dead. He was performing miracle after miracle, but they didn't see Him as the Messiah. They only saw Him as their brother and thought, *Oh, it's just Jesus. We grew up with Him.* Even when Jesus began to gain popularity, the Scripture tells us that His brothers scoffed at Him and made fun of Him. "Yeah, right. You're the Messiah!" They tried to discount Him and talk Him out of His destiny. Jesus let it go in one ear and out the other.

You can be the difference maker for your family. You can put an end to negative things that have been passed down. What you're dealing with may not have started with you, but it can stop with you. God wants you to set a new standard. You're not limited by where you came from. Just because negative things have been passed down to you doesn't mean they're supposed to continue with you. You're the one who can break the curse, break the poverty, break the depression, break the dysfunction.

You can take your family to the new level. Don't talk yourself out of it. Don't let circumstances discourage you. The odds may be against you, but the Most High God is for you. He is breathing in your direction right now. He's going to open doors that no man can shut, bring talent out of you that you hadn't known you had, and He'll cause the right people to be good to you. Opportunities are going to track you down—good breaks, freedom, and increase. You're stepping into the new level. Bondages that have held you and your family back are being broken. Now, do your part and have a new mind-set—an abundant mentality, a free mentality, a healthy mentality, a victorious mentality.

Consider This

Abraham was living in a limited environment when God told him to leave what was familiar and go to a land that He would show him. Have you ever felt God was telling you to leave behind the negative mind-sets you were raised with? Describe your experience.

....
....
....
....
....
....
....
....
....
....
....
....
....
....
....
....
....
....

What the Scriptures Say

"Enlarge the place of your tent, and let them stretch out the curtains of your dwellings; do not spare; lengthen your cords, and strengthen your stakes."

Isaiah 54:2 NKJV

The LORD had said to Abram, "Go from your country, your people and your father's household to the land I will show you. I will make you into a great nation, and I will bless you."

Genesis 12:1–2

....

....

....

....

....

....

....

....

....

....

....

....

....

....

....

....

....

Thoughts for Today

There is little difference in people, but that little difference makes a big difference. The little difference is attitude. The big difference is whether it is positive or negative.

Clement Stone

It's easy to have a great attitude when things are going our way…. It's when difficult challenges rise before us…that attitude becomes the difference maker.

John Maxwell

Faith is daring the soul to go beyond what the eyes can see.

William Clark

....

....

....

....

....

....

....

....

....

....

....

....

....

....

A Prayer for Today

Father in heaven, thank You that I can be the difference maker and take my family to a new level. Because Jesus said it was finished, the past is finished and this is a new day. Thank You for the seeds of greatness that You put in me and for the talent that You're going to bring out of me that I hadn't known I had. I declare that I am not limited by where I come from and that the negative things that were passed down to me and have held me back are being broken right now. In Jesus' Name. Amen.

....
....
....
....
....
....
....
....
....
....
....
....
....
....
....
....

Takeaway Truth

You have seeds of greatness in you.
The Most High God breathed His life into you.
Make sure your environment is not holding
you back. You need to be around people who
inspire you, people who are making a difference,
not just people who are settling for the status quo.
Tell that limited mind-set, "It is finished.
I'm dreaming big dreams. I'm praying bold
prayers. I'm expecting to go further
than how I was raised."

NEXT LEVEL
THINKING

Recognize Your Value

CHAPTER NINE

Be Secure in Who You Are

» Key Truth «

Your value is not based on what you do,
what your income is, or who you know.
Those are all superficial. Those things can
change. Your value comes from your Creator.
God breathed His life into you. You are
a child of the Most High God. You have
the DNA of Almighty God.

Too often we base our value on how someone is treating us, how successful we are, how perfect we've lived. The problem is that all those things can change. If you're trying to get your value from how people treat you, then if they hurt or disappoint you, you're going to feel devalued. If you're basing your value upon your achievements, then if something happens and you don't have those achievements, your sense of value will go down and you'll be living with insecurities, feeling inferior. That's basing your value on your performance, but here's the key: your value should be based solely on the fact that you are a child of the Most High God.

How someone treats you doesn't change your value. What they say about you or do to you doesn't lessen who you are. Mistakes you've made don't decrease your value. That's what you did; that's not who you are. You can buy a bigger house, drive a more luxurious car, and get the big promotion you've worked so hard for, but that doesn't make you more valuable. That increases your net worth, not your self-worth. You were just as valuable when you had the small apartment and no title behind your name. That position may give you more influence, but not more value. If you're a stay-at-home mom raising your children, you may not have the influence of a CEO, but you have the same value.

In Luke 4, Jesus was led by the Spirit into the wilderness, where He was tempted by the enemy three times. He'd been out there for forty days and hadn't eaten anything. The enemy said to Jesus, "If You are the Son of God, tell this stone to become bread." He was trying to get Jesus to base His value on His performance. The enemy was saying, "If You turn this stone into bread, You can prove You're the Son of God. You performed a miracle." Jesus refused to do it. He said, "Man doesn't live by bread alone." He was saying, in effect,

"I don't have to do anything to prove Who I am. I don't have to perform to feel good about Myself. I know Who I am."

The enemy couldn't deceive Jesus into basing His value upon His performance, so in the second temptation he tried to go with a possession-based value. He took Jesus to a high place and showed Him all the kingdoms of the world in a moment of time. The enemy said, "You can have it all, if You'll just bow down and worship me." Jesus answered him, "No, thanks. I don't need possessions to prove My worth and value. I don't have to have what you think is important to feel good about Who I am."

Possession-based value didn't work with Jesus, nor did performance-based value, so the enemy tried one final temptation: a popularity-based value. He took Jesus to the highest point of the temple. It was very crowded below with all kinds of people. He said, "If You are the Son of God, jump off this building. You said Your angels would protect You from any harm." He was trying to get Jesus to show off. Everybody in the temple area would see Him floating to the ground and be amazed. He'd gain instant popularity. Jesus answered the enemy again, "I don't need possessions. I don't need performance. I don't need popularity to feel valuable. I know Who I am. I'm the Son of the living God."

The enemy tried to deceive Jesus into proving who He was. Many people live in a proving mode. They can't feel good about themselves unless they prove to people that they are important, prove to their coworkers that they are talented, and prove to their critics that they really are okay. There is a constant struggle going on in their lives. They are always having to outdo, outperform, outdrive, and outdress somebody else. It's as though you're running on a treadmill that never stops. It's very freeing when you realize you don't have to prove anything to anyone. You don't have to impress people.

Consider This

We all struggle with proving ourselves. What areas of your life are you facing now that involve trying to prove yourself? What valuable lessons can you take from Jesus' example that will help keep your faith strong?

....

....

....

....

....

....

....

....

....

....

....

....

....

....

....

....

....

....

....

....

....

....

What the Scriptures Say

Am I now trying to win the approval of human beings, or of God? Or am I trying to please people? If I were still trying to please people, I would not be a servant of Christ.

Galatians 1:10

I praise you because I am fearfully and wonderfully made; your works are wonderful, I know that full well.

Psalm 139:14

....

....

....

....

....

....

....

....

....

....

....

....

....

....

....

....

....

....

Thoughts for Today

Do not let your happiness depend on something you may lose...
only (upon) the Beloved who will never pass away.

C. S. Lewis

Satan's purpose is to take from you what God has given to you.

John Osteen

My worth is what I am worth to God; and that is a
marvelous great deal, for Christ died for me.

William Temple

....

....

....

....

....

....

....

....

....

....

....

....

....

....

....

....

A Prayer for Today

Father, thank You that I can base my value solely on the fact that I am Your child rather than on my performance, and thank You that nothing that someone else says about me or does to me can change my value. Help me to know in my heart that nothing I will ever do, ever achieve, or ever overcome will make me any more valuable. Thank You that I can get off the treadmill of trying to prove myself to others. I declare that I don't have to have popularity, possessions, or performance to feel good about myself. In Jesus' Name. Amen.

Takeaway Truth

You can't get any more valuable than you already are at this very moment. You can add titles to your résumé and get more friends, but that doesn't change your value. Whether you're wearing Gucci or Goodwill, your value never changes. Say as Jesus did, "I don't have to have popularity, possessions, or performance to feel good about myself. I am secure in who I am."

CHAPTER TEN

There's Only One Whose Approval Really Matters

›› *Key Truth* ‹‹

When you base your value on what God says about you, it's going to lift you up. He says you're amazing and that you're the apple of His eye. Receive your approval from Him. He loves you just the way He made you. You don't have to have other people's approval to be happy. God approves you. He's the only One Who really matters.

When Jesus was riding into Jerusalem on a young donkey to celebrate the Passover feast, a large crowd of people celebrated His arrival, shouting, "Hosanna! Blessed is He who comes in the name of the Lord!" They were so excited to see Him. He received a hero's welcome. But a few days later, those same people, instead of shouting, "Hosanna!" were shouting, "Crucify Him! We don't want Him here!" When Jesus went to trial and needed His closest friends to support Him, most of His disciples, the ones He had poured His life into, weren't anywhere around. When He asked them to stay up and pray, they fell asleep.

If you base your value on people's support, how much they approve you and encourage you, then if for some reason they stop doing that, you'll feel devalued. As long as they're telling you, "You're great," you'll feel great. The problem is, if they change their minds and stop telling you that, you're not going to feel great. You can't base your value on what people give or don't give you. People are often unreliable. One day, they'll say, "You're beautiful," and the next, "I don't care for you." "Hosanna!" on Palm Sunday, and "Crucify Him!" on Good Friday.

If you don't know who you are without other people, then if they leave, you'll be lost. They'll take you with them, because your identity was caught up in who they made you to be. Then you'll have to try to find somebody else to tell you who you are. But you don't need other people to tell you who you are. People will let you down. People will get jealous. People have their own issues. Let your heavenly Father tell you who you are. Get your value, your self-worth, your approval from Him. He says you're a masterpiece. He says you're one of a kind, a prized possession.

Somebody may have told you the opposite. "You're not talented."

"You're not attractive." "You don't have a good personality." Let that go in one ear and out the other. They don't determine your value. What they say or do to you doesn't make you any less a masterpiece. Quit letting how people treat you make you feel inferior. They don't control your destiny. They didn't breathe life into you. They didn't approve you. Your value came from your Creator, from the God Who spoke worlds into existence. The good news is they can't change your value, and you can't change it either. God put it in you before you showed up. You don't need their approval. Don't give away your power. Don't put your identity, your value, into somebody else's hands.

Even good people who love you very much can't give you everything you need. They cannot keep you approved, validated, and feeling secure. You have to go to your heavenly Father. Sometimes we're putting pressure on people to keep us fixed, to keep us feeling validated. Let them off the hook. They're not your Savior. You already have a Savior. He's on the throne. Go to Him and not to people. You belong to Him and not to them. You don't have to prove anything. You don't have to try to impress people or get value from them. Just be who you are. Be amazing.

Consider This

Describe a time in your life when you based your value on people's support, how much they approved you, and then they stopped doing that. How did it impact you? As you look back on that experience, what did you learn from it?

....
....
....
....
....
....
....
....
....
....
....
....
....
....
....
....
....
....
....
....

What the Scriptures Say

The fear of human opinion disables; trusting in GOD
protects you from that.

For we are God's masterpiece. He has created us anew in Christ
Jesus, so we can do the good things he planned for us long ago.

....

....

....

....

....

....

....

....

....

....

....

....

....

....

....

....

....

Thoughts for Today

Approval addiction is essentially an act of self-abandonment. Instead of finding your value and worth from your Creator, you have given your heart up for adoption. You have given it away to others for love and approval, making them responsible for your feelings. Depending on anyone other than God for fundamental validation is just asking for heartbreak.

Pete Wilson

Don't seek to be a people pleaser...don't compromise what you know is right in your heart to gain the approval of others. The only approval you need is God's, and you already have that.

Joyce Meyer

If you are not feeding your soul on the realities of the presence, promises, and provisions of Christ, you will ask the people, situations, and things around you to be the messiah that they can never be. If you are not attaching your identity to the unshakable love of your Savior, you will ask the things in your life to be your Savior, and it will never happen.

Paul Tripp

....

....

....

....

....

....

....

....

A Prayer for Today

Father in heaven, thank You that whether or not anyone else ever approves me, the fact is that I have received my approval from You, and You are the only One Who truly matters. Thank You that You love me just as You made me and that my name is engraved on the palms of Your hands. Help me to never allow others to make me feel insignificant. I declare that I belong to You, and I won't give away my power and put my identity, my value, into somebody else's hands. In Jesus' Name. Amen.

....

....

....

....

....

....

....

....

....

....

....

....

....

....

....

....

....

Takeaway Truth

If you're going to recognize your value,
you have to see yourself as amazing,
as wonderful. It's not because of who you are,
but because of Who made you. All through
the day, despite what your thoughts are telling
you, despite who left you out or said something
negative about you, you need to remind yourself,
"I am amazing. I am a masterpiece. I have
been wonderfully made."

NEXT LEVEL
THINKING

Live with the Boldness of a Son

CHAPTER ELEVEN

Get Rid of a Slave Mentality

›› *Key Truth* ‹‹

Because of negative things in the past
or even mistakes we've made, it's easy to
forget who we really are. The Scripture says,
"Beloved, now are you the sons of God."
Too often we live as though we're a slave to
an addiction, to mediocrity, to others' approval.
You may have a lot coming against you,
but you are not a slave, you are a son.

The Israelites had been in slavery in Egypt for four hundred years. They were mistreated and taken advantage of. God saw the injustice and sent plagues on the Pharaoh and his people until Pharaoh finally decided to let them go. When the Israelites headed out toward the Promised Land, they were excited that their dream of freedom had finally come true...until Pharaoh came chasing after them. He took six hundred of his fastest chariots and was quickly approaching as the Israelites came to a dead end at the Red Sea. Pharaoh was saying, in effect, "You're my slaves. I own you, and I'm taking you back." God was saying, "You're my sons and daughters. I've redeemed you. I'm taking you forward into freedom." I can imagine that this debate was playing back and forth in the minds of the Israelites. "You're a son" or "You're a slave."

That same debate is taking place about you. One voice is saying, "You're a slave. You'll never get well. You'll always struggle in your finances. You'll always be addicted." But God is saying, "You're a son. I've equipped you, empowered you, and anointed you." Now, you get to choose which way you go. If you believe the lie that you're a slave, that you've reached your limits, it will keep you from your purpose. You need to rise up and say, "I'm a son. I'm not a slave to my past or to the people who hurt me. I'm not a slave to any negative thing. I'm a child of the Most High God."

This is what happened to the Israelites. They saw God free them from slavery through supernatural plagues and deliver them from the Pharaoh and his army at the Red Sea. They saw God provide them with manna to eat and bring water out of a rock in the wilderness. When they came to the border of the Promised Land, you would think they would be full of faith. But when the ten spies saw how big the people were, they told Moses, "They're too powerful for us. Let's just go back to Egypt and be slaves." They had been in slavery for so long that they never quit seeing themselves as slaves. God brought them out of slavery, but slavery never got out of them.

You may have struggled in an area for a long time, but don't have a limited mind-set. You have to give God permission to increase you. It starts in your thinking. You can't see yourself as a slave and enjoy the blessings of a son. If you grew up in lack, not having enough, surrounded by mediocrity, don't let that poverty spirit get in or stay in you. That is not who you are. You're the one to break the curse. You're the one to set a new standard. God is about to loose resources, promotion, ideas, and opportunities for you. Have a vision for increase. See yourself as a son rising higher. You have seeds of greatness. You are not limited by how you were raised, by your family, by what you didn't get.

Stop thinking like a slave and start thinking like a son. Stop thinking about what you were, what you've been through, and the mistakes you've made. Rather, start thinking about who you are—you are free, you are blessed, you are a masterpiece, you are victorious.

Consider This

It is never easy to admit we have a slave mentality in areas of our lives, but as long as we allow it to remain, it will limit our life. Take some time and reflect on what those areas have been in your life. What truth about God will keep you from being a slave to them?

....
....
....
....
....
....
....
....
....
....
....
....
....
....
....
....
....
....
....

What the Scriptures Say

Dear friends, now we are the children of God, and what we will be has not yet been made known. But we know that when Christ appears, we shall be like him, for we shall see him as he is.

1 John 3:2

"So if the Son makes you free, then you are unquestionably free."

John 8:36 AMP

....
....
....
....
....
....
....
....
....
....
....
....
....
....
....
....
....

Thoughts for Today

Sonship is a heart that feels at rest and secure in God's love; it believes it belongs, it is free from shame and self-condemnation, it walks in honor toward all people, and it is willing to humble itself before man and God.

Jack Frost

Your life today is a result of your thinking yesterday. Your life tomorrow will be determined by what you think today.

John Maxwell

However many blessings we expect from God, His infinite liberality will always exceed all our wishes and our thoughts.

John Calvin

....
....
....
....
....
....
....
....
....
....
....
....
....
....

A Prayer for Today

Father, thank You that I am not a slave to my past or to people who hurt me, because I was bought with a precious price and I belong to You as Your child. Thank You that I am free, I am whole, favor surrounds me, and Your goodness and mercy follow me wherever I go. Help me to have a vision for increase and abundance and to know that You are breaking all the bondages that have held me back. I declare that the enemy has been defeated and has no power over me. I am a son of the living God. In Jesus' Name. Amen.

Takeaway Truth

God has not only freed us from sin, from guilt,
from depression, and from sicknesses,
but He took care of our enemy. You don't
have to live with the threat that you might be
recaptured. Your oppressor has been defeated;
the enemy has no power over you. You're
not a runaway slave, you're a son of the
Most High God. Have a son mentality,
an abundant mentality.

CHAPTER TWELVE

You Are a Son Right Now

» Key Truth «

The Scripture tells us to come boldly to the throne of grace, not as a servant saying, "God, I know I don't deserve it." If you want to put a smile on God's face, go to Him with boldness, like you know you deserve to be there and that He wants to be good to you. You don't have to earn God's love. You don't have to work for His approval.

n the story of the prodigal son in Luke 15, the young man asked his father for his inheritance and left home. He wasted all the money through partying, wild living, and making poor choices. Once he was broke, he was so desperate that he ended up working in a farmer's field, feeding the hogs. When he finally came to his senses, he thought, *The servants at home live better than I do. I'm going to go back to my father's house, and after all the wrongs I've done, I know I can't live at home, but maybe my father will hire me as one of his servants.* Because of his mistakes, he stopped seeing himself as a son and saw himself as a servant. He didn't think he had a right to be in the family anymore.

How many of us have disqualified ourselves from God's goodness? We knew at one time we were a son, at one time we knew God was going to help us, favor us, and bless us, but we made poor choices. We got off course. Now we believe the lie that somehow we've gone from a son to a slave, that God won't have anything to do with us.

This young man got his nerve up and headed back home. He was prepared for his father to let him have it, to say, "Don't even think about coming on this property." But as he got closer, he could see his father standing at the end of the driveway, as though he had been waiting for him. All of a sudden, his father started running toward him, grabbed him, and started hugging and kissing him. The son said, "Dad, I don't deserve to be called your son, but maybe you will hire me as a servant." His father stopped him and said, "What are you talking about? Don't you know you're my son, and you'll always be my son?" There's nothing you can do to change the fact that you're a son. When you gave your life to Christ, you were born into the family of God. You can't get unborn. You can't get too far off course. You may disqualify yourself, but God never disqualifies you.

Are you living like a slave when in fact you're a son? Are you trying to convince God to hire you as a servant when God is saying, "Kill the fatted calf! My son is home"? God has already received you back into His family. But what if the son had said, "Dad, I can't accept your goodness. Let me just work to pay you back the inheritance I wasted"? That would have ruined the story. Yet how many of us are doing the same thing? We're not receiving God's goodness. We're beating ourselves up for our failures. We're letting the accuser convince us that we've somehow gone from a son to a slave.

When this son returned home, the father never brought up his past failures. He didn't say, "I'll let you come back, but you shouldn't have done that." God is not interested in your past. The enemy will work overtime trying to remind you of all your mistakes, making you feel guilty and unworthy. Don't believe those lies. You're not going to qualify as a son when you perform well enough. You're a son right now. Why don't you come back into the family, start believing again, start dreaming again? You can cause God to turn on the music and start a party up in heaven. When He sees you shake off a slave mentality and start having a son mentality, He says about you, "Go kill the fatted calf. We're going to have a party. My son, my daughter, has come back home."

Consider This

What is God showing you about Himself through the example of the prodigal's father? What message of hope do you feel God is personally speaking to your heart?

....
....
....
....
....
....
....
....
....
....
....
....
....
....
....
....
....
....
....
....
....
....

What the Scriptures Say

"It is your Father's good pleasure to give you the kingdom."

Luke 12:32 NKJV

"The father said to his servants, 'Quick! Bring the best robe and put it on him. Put a ring on his finger and sandals on his feet. Bring the fattened calf and kill it. Let's have a feast and celebrate. For this son of mine was dead and is alive again; he was lost and is found.' So they began to celebrate."

Luke 15:22–24

....

....

....

....

....

....

....

....

....

....

....

....

....

....

....

....

Thoughts for Today

"Father" is the most significant name of the God of the Bible. It is the name that sets Christianity apart from all the other religions of the world, inviting us to believe in a Son and to enter into an intimate family relationship with a loving Father. Jesus, the Son of God, came so that we could meet His Father, be adopted into the family of God, and relate to the Almighty God of the universe in an intimate, personal, concrete way as sons and daughters.

Mary Kassian

Because of fear, I had forfeited strength, life, and beauty. I had lost a sense of my true self, and with that loss so much of what God wanted for me was yet unrealized.

Lisa Bevere

Pray for great things, expect great things, work for great things, but above all, pray.

R. A. Torrey

A Prayer for Today

Father in heaven, thank You that I can come boldly to Your throne of grace knowing that I don't have to earn Your love or work for Your approval or pay You back for my mistakes. Thank You that the price has been paid and I've been born into Your royal family and a brand-new life. I ask You to give me the kingdom, just as You promised, knowing that You are pleased with me as Your child. I believe that You are longing to show Your goodness to me and to make me into Your masterpiece. In Jesus' Name. Amen.

....
....
....
....
....
....
....
....
....
....
....
....
....
....
....
....

Takeaway Truth

Sometimes what's holding us back is that we think we're average, just ordinary, when in fact we are royalty. We are sons and daughters of the Most High God. When God breathed His life into you, He crowned you with His favor. He put a robe of righteousness on you. He says, "You have been fearfully and wonderfully made." Now, do your part, shake off the slave mentality, and start having a son mentality.

NEXT LEVEL
THINKING

Know You Are Loved

CHAPTER THIRTEEN

You Are the One Whom He Loves

» *Key Truth* «

God doesn't love you because you're religious or good enough. He loves you because you are His child. When you receive His love, you'll live with a confidence. When you go from "I think" to "I know," you'll quit trying to earn His love. You'll quit trying to be good enough. You'll live securely, knowing that your heavenly Father loves you.

When you *know* that somebody loves you, it puts you at ease. You don't have to try to perform, to impress, to be good enough. You can relax and be yourself. You're secure. But a lot of people live with an "I *think* He loves me" mentality when it comes to God, because they base it on their performance. "I went to church last weekend. I resisted temptation. I did good. I think He loves me." The problem with this approach is that when we don't perform perfectly, we think God changes His mind about us.

Sometimes we're trying to clean ourselves up, trying hard to be good enough, and then we'll believe that God really loves us. But God loves you right now. He loved you when you were doing wrong and off course. He still loves you. The apostle Paul says that "*nothing* will ever be able to separate us from the love of God." God put His love on you permanently. Quit trying to earn His love. There's nothing you can do to make God love you any more or any less. It's a gift. Just receive it by faith.

First John 3:1 speaks of "the great love" with which God loved us. It wasn't a little love, an "I think" love, or a conditional love. It was and is a great love. We think about how much we love God, but what's far more profound is how much God loves us. Before you were formed in your mother's womb, God knew you. He took time to plan out all your days. He knows your thoughts before you think them. He knows your words before you speak them.

In the Bible, the book of John was written by the disciple John. What's interesting is that within this book he never refers to himself as John. When he talks about himself, instead of using his name, five times he referred to himself as "the disciple whom Jesus loved" (John 13:23). When Matthew, Mark, and Luke wrote their books, their accounts of the gospel, they referred to themselves by using their own names. Can you imagine if they had read John's account? They would've thought, *Who does John think he is, describing himself as the one whom Jesus loved? Jesus loved us all. The nerve of that guy.* But John had an incredible confidence not just in how much he loved God, but in how much God loved him.

In John 19, John wrote, "When Jesus saw His mother, and the disciple whom Jesus loved standing by." Now, you know that Jesus probably loved His mother more than He loved John. But John didn't tell us how much Jesus loved His mother, he just reiterated the fact that he was the one whom Jesus loved. Some may fault John as being arrogant and self-centered, but John knew how much God loved him and was secure in His love.

When you can do as John did, you'll go to Him with confidence, you'll "come boldly to the throne of grace" (Heb. 4:16 NKJV). You'll pray bold prayers, you'll ask Him for your dreams, you'll believe for your health to turn around, you'll expect new doors to open—not because of who you are, but because of Who your Father is. You can wake up in the morning and say in your heart, "Good morning, Lord. It's me, the one whom You love." All through the day you can say, "Lord, I love You, and I know I'm the one whom You love."

Consider This

Why do a lot of people live with an "I *think* God loves me" mentality? Have you struggled with the thought that God loves you conditionally? Describe examples from your past experiences.

....

....

....

....

....

....

....

....

....

....

....

....

....

....

....

....

....

....

....

....

What the Scriptures Say

For I am convinced that neither death nor life, neither angels nor demons, neither the present nor the future, nor any powers, neither height nor depth, nor anything else in all creation, will be able to separate us from the love of God that is in Christ Jesus our Lord.

Romans 8:38–39

See what great love the Father has lavished on us, that we should be called children of God! And that is what we are!

1 John 3:1

Thoughts for Today

Believe God's love and power more than you believe your own feelings and experiences. Your rock is Christ, and it is not the rock that ebbs and flows but the sea.

Samuel Rutherford

God loves each of us as if there were only one of us.

Augustine

There is no need to plead that the love of God shall fill our heart as though He were unwilling to fill us; He is willing as light is willing to flood a room that is opened to its brightness; willing as water is willing to flow into an emptied channel. Love is pressing round us on all sides like air. Cease to resist, and instantly love takes possession.

Amy Carmichael

....

....

....

....

....

....

....

....

....

....

....

....

....

A Prayer for Today

Father in heaven, thank You that Your love is a gift, and there is nothing I can do to make You love me any more or any less. Thank You that You don't love me because I'm religious, or I'm good enough, or I come from a certain family. You love me because I am Your child. Help me to get rid of the "I think You love me" mentality and start having an "I know You love me" mentality. I believe and declare that I am the one whom You love and nothing can ever separate me from Your love. In Jesus' Name. Amen.

....

....

....

....

....

....

....

....

....

....

....

....

....

....

....

....

Takeaway Truth

If you want to make God smile,
start approaching Him like you know
He loves you, like you know He's for you,
like you know He's longing to be good to you.
It doesn't bring God any pleasure when we
go around feeling insecure and unworthy,
and beating ourselves up for past mistakes.
Nothing you can do will make God love
you more. You are His favorite. You're
the one whom He loves.

CHAPTER FOURTEEN

This Is Real Love

» Key Truth «

Real love is not our love for God, it's God's love for us. When we try to perform to gain His love, the problem is that we can never measure up. There will always be something we can't do right, some reason we can't feel good about ourselves. Why don't you take the pressure off and receive real love, God's love for you?

First John 4:10 says, "This is real love—not that we loved God, but that He loved us and sent His Son as a sacrifice to take away our sins." Real love is not our love for God, it's God's love for us. When we try to perform to gain His love, the problem is that we can never measure up. There will always be some reason we can't feel good about ourselves. Why don't you take the pressure off and receive real love, God's love for you?

That's what the lady who was caught in the act of adultery had to do in John 8. The religious leaders brought her to Jesus and said, "Teacher, in the law Moses commanded us to stone such women. What do You say we should do?" Jesus answered, "You who are without sin throw the first stone." Starting with the oldest ones first, they all left. Jesus asked the woman, "Where are your accusers? Hasn't anyone condemned you?" She said, "No one, Lord." He said, "Neither do I condemn you; go and sin no more." He didn't say, "Go and sin no more, and then I won't condemn you. Change your ways, get your act together, quit giving in to the temptation, and then I'll love you." Just the opposite. He first said, "I don't condemn you." Before He talked about her behavior, Jesus wanted to make sure she knew she was the one whom He loved.

When she felt this real love, when she realized the one person who could have condemned her wouldn't do it, I believe something happened on the inside. She walked out of the temple a changed woman. Sometimes religion tells us, "Clean yourself up, then God will love you. If you fail to do what's right, if you don't perform correctly, God won't have anything to do with you. If you're good enough, if you measure up, then God will help you." That's not real love; that's conditional love. Real love is not about your performance, what you do or don't do. It's about what God has already done. It's not based on how much you love God; it's based on how much God loves you.

When my brother, Paul, was little, my parents would put him in his bed at night, and then they would go and get in their own bed. Their rooms were just a few feet apart, down a short hallway. My father would always say, "Good night, Paul," and Paul would answer back, "Good night, Daddy. Good night, Mother." One night, after they had said their good-nights, Paul was a little afraid and said, "Daddy, are you still in there?" My father said, "Yes, Paul, I'm still here." A few seconds later, Paul asked, "Daddy, is your face turned toward me?" My father said, "Yes, my face is turned toward you." Somehow, it made Paul feel better just knowing that our father's face was turned toward him.

Can I tell you that your heavenly Father's face is always turned toward you? You're the one whom He loves. You're His favorite child. He's not counting your mistakes against you. Receive His love. All through the day, say, "Lord, thank You that I'm the one whom You love. Thank You that Your face is turned toward me." Remember, real love is not about your love for God; it's recognizing the great love God has for you. If you do this, I believe and declare you're going to live confidently and securely, overcoming obstacles, rising higher, and becoming everything He's created you to be.

Consider This

Read the story in John 8:1–11 about the lady who was caught in the act of adultery. When her accusers had left, what did Jesus not say to her, and what did He say to her? What message of hope do you feel God is personally speaking to your heart through her story?

....
....
....
....
....
....
....
....
....
....
....
....
....
....
....
....
....
....
....
....

What the Scriptures Say

And so we know and rely on the love God has for us. God is love.

1 John 4:16

"I have loved you with an everlasting love; I have drawn you with unfailing kindness."

Jeremiah 31:3

....
....
....
....
....
....
....
....
....
....
....
....
....
....
....
....
....
....
....

Thoughts for Today

Trust God's love. His perfect love. Don't fear He will discover your past. He already has. Don't fear disappointing Him in the future. He can show you the chapter in which you will. With perfect knowledge of the past and perfect vision of the future, He loves you perfectly in spite of both.

Max Lucado

Life is too short, the world is too big, and God's love is too great to live ordinary.

Christine Caine

God's love for me is perfect because it's based on Him, not on me. So even when I failed, He kept loving me.

Joyce Meyer

....
....
....
....
....
....
....
....
....
....
....
....
....

A Prayer for Today

Father in heaven, thank You that real love is not about my love for You; it's recognizing the great love You have for me and resting secure in what You have already done. Thank You that I don't have to clean myself up or start performing perfectly to get You to love me. I receive Your unconditional, unlimited love as my Father. I believe that Your face is turned toward me because You are love, and I declare that I am going to live confidently and securely and become everything You've created me to be. In Jesus' Name. Amen.

Takeaway Truth

Sometimes religion tells us, "Clean yourself up, then God will love you. If you're good enough, if you measure up, then God will help you." That's not real love; that's conditional love. Real love is not about your performance, what you do or don't do. It's about what God has already done. It's not based on how much you love God; it's based on how much God loves you.

NEXT LEVEL
THINKING

Approve Yourself

CHAPTER FIFTEEN

Be Happy with Who You Are

» *Key Truth* «

You may have some weaknesses—we all do. But you're not supposed to go through life feeling wrong about yourself. You're not a finished product. God is still working on you. The Scripture speaks of how God changes us from glory to glory. You have to learn to enjoy the glory you're in right now and to feel good about yourself right where you are.

Too many people go around feeling as though something is wrong on the inside. They don't really like who they are. They focus on their faults and weaknesses. They're constantly critical toward themselves. There's a recording of everything they've done wrong that is always playing in their mind. They wonder why they're unhappy and don't realize it's because they have a war going on inside.

Here's the key: you're not a finished product. God is still working on you. The Scripture speaks of how God changes us from glory to glory. You have to learn to enjoy the glory you're in right now. You may have some weaknesses—we all do. There may be some areas where you know you need to improve, but being down on yourself is not going to help you do better. Having that nagging feeling that tells you, "You don't measure up. God's not pleased with you. You'll never get it right," is not going to help you move forward. You have to accept yourself right where you are, faults and all. God is the Potter, we are the clay. He's the one Who is making and molding you. It may not be happening as fast as you would like, but you don't control the timetable. Will you trust Him in the process? Will you accept yourself in the glory you're in right now?

The Scripture says in Hebrews 12:2, "[Looking away from all that will distract us and] focusing our eyes on Jesus, who is the Author and Perfecter of faith" (AMP). You have to look away from your faults, look away from your shortcomings. Focusing on your weaknesses will distract you from your purpose. Always thinking about how you don't measure up will distract you from the good things God has in store. This doesn't mean we don't try to improve. It means you don't let that heaviness weigh you down to where you think there's something wrong with you.

One of the worst mistakes you can make is to go through life being against yourself. Some people live with that nagging feeling that's always telling them, "You're not good enough. You'll never get it right." They've heard that playing in their minds for so long that it's become normal. Why don't you turn off that negative recording? Why don't you quit thinking about everything that's wrong with you and start thinking about what's right with you? You may have some areas in which you still struggle—we all do. No one is perfect. It's okay to feel good about who you are while you're in the process of changing.

Now, when you do this, don't be surprised if every voice tells you, "You're a hypocrite. You can't feel good about yourself. You still struggle, you still have that weakness." This is when you must have the boldness to say, "Yes, that's true, but I'm on the Potter's wheel. I'm growing and I'm changing. In the meantime, I feel good about me." Your destiny is too important to let that heaviness weigh you down. Your time is too valuable to be sitting around thinking about everything that's wrong with you. That's taking away your joy, your energy, your creativity, and your anointing. Start looking away from all of that. You're on the Potter's wheel. You're not going to change overnight. It's going to happen little by little.

Consider This

What areas of your life are you facing that you find easy to
stay negative toward yourself because you can't get them right?
Instead of beating yourself up, what attitude do you need
to take that will allow God to work?

....
....
....
....
....
....
....
....
....
....
....
....
....
....
....
....
....
....

What the Scriptures Say

Yet you, LORD, are our Father. We are the clay, you are the
potter; we are all the work of your hand.... Does the clay
say to the potter, "What are you making?"

Isaiah 64:8; 45:9

And I am convinced and sure of this very thing, that He Who
began a good work in you will continue until the day of Jesus Christ
[right up to the time of His return], developing [that good work]
and perfecting and bringing it to full completion in you.

Philippians 1:6 AMPC

Thoughts for Today

I would rather be what God chose to make me than the most glorious creature that I could think of; for to have been thought about, born in God's thought, and then made by God, is the dearest, grandest, and most precious thing in all thinking.

George MacDonald

Real contentment must come from within. You and I cannot change or control the world around us, but we can change and control the world within us.

Warren Wiersbe

Endurance is not just the ability to bear a hard thing, but to turn it into glory.

William Barclay

....
....
....
....
....
....
....
....
....
....
....
....
....

A Prayer for Today

Father in heaven, thank You that though I'm not a finished product and have some flaws, You are still working on me, changing me from glory to glory. Thank You that I don't need to stay down on myself when I can't seem to get it right or measure up, but I can be thankful for the glory I'm in right now. You are the Potter, and while You're changing me, I'm going to keep my eyes focused on Jesus and feel good about myself. I believe that I'm a work in progress, and You will get me to where I'm supposed to be. In Jesus' Name. Amen.

Takeaway Truth

If you're going to live in victory, you have to put your foot down and say, "That's it. I'm done being against myself. I'm done focusing on my weaknesses. I know I'm a child of the Most High God. I am redeemed, restored, and forgiven. God is taking me from glory to glory, so I'm going to look away from all that distracts. And I'm going to enjoy the glory I'm in right now."

CHAPTER SIXTEEN

You Are Already Approved

» *Key Truth* «

When you understand that the Creator of the universe approves you, you won't go around being down on yourself because you're not where you thought you should be, trying to gain God's approval by performing perfectly, never making a mistake. You know God's approval is not based on how good you are. It's based on how good He is.

od says, "Before I formed you in the womb I knew you [and approved of you as My chosen instrument]" (Jer. 1:5 AMP). It doesn't say, "He approves you as long as you don't make any mistakes and don't have any weaknesses." He approved you before you were formed in your mother's womb. This means He approves you with your weaknesses and despite those shortcomings. He knows the end from the beginning. He knew every area in which you would ever struggle. That's why He has you on the Potter's wheel and is changing you from glory to glory. You're not defective, you're not a mistake. When God created you, He called you a masterpiece. He stepped back and said, "That was very good."

You may have flaws and weaknesses. Those voices will try to convince you to live feeling down on yourself, thinking, *God's not going to bless me. You don't know what I struggle with. I'll never get it right.* Don't believe those lies. Before you showed up on planet earth, God already approved you. Since God approves you, why don't you start approving yourself? Why don't you start feeling good about who you are? His approval is not based on your performance, it's based on your relationship. He handpicked you. He chose you before you could choose Him.

The apostle Paul says to put on "the breastplate of God's approval" (Eph. 6:14 TLB). Every morning when you get up, you should say, "Father, thank You that You approve me. Thank You that You are pleased with me." You have to put it on. It's not going to happen automatically. If you're not putting His approval on, you'll start living with guilt, feeling unworthy. It's a breastplate, meaning that it covers the most important area of your life, which is your heart. You may have many areas in which you still struggle, but being against yourself is not going to help you do better. You have to put on His approval. All through the day in your thoughts be saying, "God is pleased with me. He's at work in my life. I'm not perfect, but I'm forgiven. I have these weaknesses, but I'm on the Potter's wheel. He's making me, He's molding me. I'm coming up higher."

The most important relationship you have is your relationship with yourself. If you don't get along with yourself, if you don't like yourself, you won't be able to get along with anybody else. Jesus says, "Love your neighbor as yourself" (Matt. 22:39). You can't love your neighbor if you don't first love yourself. You can't give away something you don't have. If you don't have a healthy respect for yourself, if you're not putting on His approval each day, you'll start focusing on your faults and shortcomings. You'll end up feeling insecure and inferior. That will cause you to struggle in relationships.

Some people have never once said, "I like myself. I like my gifts, my personality, my looks. I'm happy with who God made me to be." You may say, "Well, I'm not going to say I like myself. That's weird." But if you don't like yourself in a healthy way, you will project inferiority, unfriendliness, and discontentment to others. I'm asking you to feel good about who you are. God is changing you from glory to glory. Start enjoying the glory that you're in right now. Don't you dare go through life being against yourself.

Consider This

To put on "the breastplate of God's approval" does not happen automatically. Write out some specific ways that you need to start approving yourself.

....

....

....

....

....

....

....

....

....

....

....

....

....

....

....

....

....

....

....

....

What the Scriptures Say

"This is My beloved Son, in whom I am well pleased."

Matthew 3:17 NKJV

So, as God's own chosen people, who are holy [set apart, sanctified
for His purpose] and well-beloved [by God Himself], put on
a heart of compassion, kindness, humility, gentleness, and
patience [which has the power to endure whatever injustice
or unpleasantness comes, with good temper].

Colossians 3:12 AMP

Thoughts for Today

God's love sets us free from the need to seek approval. Knowing that we are loved by God, accepted by God, approved by God, and that we are new creations in Christ empowers us to reject self-rejection and embrace a healthy self-love. Being secure in God's love for us, our love for Him, and our love for ourselves, prepares us to fulfill the second greatest commandment: to love our neighbor as ourselves.

Myles Monroe

Our desire for approval can only truly be met by receiving God's acceptance and approval of us.

Joyce Meyer

Your approval before God is woven into the life and sacrifice of Jesus Christ on the cross, not what other men and women think about you.

Matt Chandler

....
....
....
....
....
....
....
....
....
....
....

A Prayer for Today

Father in heaven, thank You that I can take off the rags of condemnation, unworthiness, and guilt over my shortcomings and failures and put on the breastplate of Your approval, knowing that You are pleased with me. Thank You that You chose me and loved me long before I had done anything right or wrong, before there was any performance on my part to base it upon. I declare that I am happy with who You made me to be and I am done with being against myself. In Jesus' Name. Amen.

....

....

....

....

....

....

....

....

....

....

....

....

....

....

....

....

....

Takeaway Truth

Something powerful happens when you say, "I like who I am. I'm not perfect, and I have some shortcomings, but I'm growing, I'm changing. And since God approves me, I'm going to approve myself." When you do this, chains are broken in the unseen realm— chains of guilt, chains of low self-esteem, chains of inferiority. When you are for yourself, you are in agreement with God.

NEXT LEVEL
THINKING

Get the Contaminants Out

CHAPTER SEVENTEEN

Guard Your Heart

›› *Key Truth* ‹‹

One of our most important responsibilities is to keep our heart pure. Life is too short to live offended over the past, not forgiving someone, bitter over what didn't work out. You have to guard your heart. It's easy to let what's on the outside get on the inside. It takes discipline to say, "God, I'm turning this over to You. I'm not going to dwell on the past."

don't know about you, but I've found bitterness is always knocking at the door—people do you wrong, you didn't get the promotion, you came down with an illness. You can't stop difficult things from happening to you, but you can choose how you respond to them. If you hold on to the hurt and dwell on the offense, you open the door to bitterness. When you're bitter, it affects every area of your life. Bitterness poisons your attitude to the point where you see everything in a negative light.

I know people who are still bitter over something that happened thirty years ago. They're bitter because they were mistreated growing up or because a relationship didn't work out. You have to let it go. God sees what's happening to you. He knows what wasn't fair, He knows who walked away, and He knows how to make it up to you. He knows how to bring you out better. Let it go and trust Him to be your vindicator. The longer you hold on to it, the harder it is to get rid of it. The more you dwell on it, the more you relive it, the more you let it bother you, the deeper it gets rooted in you.

Here's how bitterness tries to get inside. When you don't get the contract you work so hard for, bitterness will come and say, "That's not fair. Go ahead and have a chip on your shoulder." At the office a coworker says something to try to make you look bad in front of your boss. It starts off as a small offense, not a big deal, just a little seed. If you choose to ignore it and let it go, nothing will come of it. But if you dwell on it, if you start thinking of how you can pay them back, the next time you see them you'll give them the cold shoulder. Now that little seed is taking root. Before long, it will grow and pollute other areas of your life.

That's why it says in Scripture, "See to it that...no 'root of bitterness' springs up and causes trouble, and by it many become defiled" (Heb. 12:15 ESV). Notice that bitterness is described as a root. You can't see a root; it's underground. But the bitter root produces bitter fruit. If you have a root of bitterness, it will contaminate your life.

Proverbs 4:23 says, "Guard your heart with all vigilance...for out of it flow the springs of life" (AMPC). One of our most important responsibilities is to keep our heart pure. It's easy to let what's on the outside get on the inside. It takes discipline to say, "I'm not going to dwell on that offense. I'm not going to feel sorry for myself because something didn't work out." You only have so much emotional energy each day. It's not an unlimited supply. Do you know how much energy it takes to hold a grudge, to go around offended? That's wasting valuable energy that you need for your dreams, for your children, and for your destiny.

The good news is, you don't have to live with bitter roots. Ask God to show you what's causing you to be bitter. Maybe you need to forgive somebody, or maybe you're still beating yourself up over a mistake you made. Be honest with yourself and say, "God, help me to get rid of this root of bitterness. I don't want to be bitter. I want my passion back. I want to love again, to dream again. Help me to let it go and move up to the next level."

Consider This

Have you ever felt bitter about something difficult that's happened to you? Describe your experience and how it affected your relationships, your joy, and your dreams.

....
....
....
....
....
....
....
....
....
....
....
....
....
....
....
....
....
....
....
....
....
....
....

What the Scriptures Say

Get rid of all bitterness, rage and anger, brawling and slander, along with every form of malice.

Ephesians 4:31

But I am afraid that just as Eve was deceived by the serpent's cunning, your minds may somehow be led astray from your sincere and pure devotion to Christ.

2 Corinthians 11:3

....

....

....

....

....

....

....

....

....

....

....

....

....

....

Thoughts for Today

Acrid bitterness inevitably seeps into the lives of people who harbor grudges and suppress anger, and bitterness is always a poison. It keeps your pain alive instead of letting you deal with it and get beyond it. Bitterness sentences you to relive the hurt over and over.

Lee Strobel

God has a big eraser.

Billy Zeoli

Forgiveness is the economy of the heart. Forgiveness saves the expense of anger, the cost of hatred, the waste of spirits.

Hannah More

....

....

....

....

....

....

....

....

....

....

....

....

....

....

A Prayer for Today

Father, thank You that because Jesus said, "It is finished," He made a way for my heart to be pure of all the contaminants that try to get in it from the outside. Thank You that it is possible to keep my heart free from any roots of bitterness. Search my heart and show me if there is anything rooted from my past that needs to be gotten rid of, any unforgiveness or anger or sourness, and help me to release it. I believe that You are my vindicator and that what was meant for my harm You will use to my advantage. In Jesus' Name. Amen.

Takeaway Truth

Don't let a bitter root contaminate your life.
It's time to move forward. It's very freeing when
you can let things go and say, "God, they did
me wrong, but You are my vindicator. I had
a disappointment, but I know that You'll turn
what was meant for my harm and use it to my
advantage." That's how you beat bitterness:
you guard your heart. You don't let what's
on the outside get on the inside.

CHAPTER EIGHTEEN

God Is Not in Your Past

» *Key Truth* «

Sometimes life doesn't seem fair. You can have more than your share of bad breaks, but God promises He will give you grace for every season. What you're going through may not be good, but God knows how to bring good out of it. You've haven't seen your best days. God is not finished with you. The enemy doesn't have the final say; God does.

n Mark 16, Jesus had been crucified and His body was laid in a tomb. When Mary Magdalene and two other women went to the tomb early the next morning, they found the stone had been rolled away. They went into the tomb and saw an angel, which frightened them. He said to them, "You're looking for Jesus, but He is not here. He has risen! He is going ahead of you into Galilee. There you will see Him." Notice that the angel said, "He is not *here*. He is *there*." The angel was saying, in effect, "I know this looks bad. I know you're disappointed, but don't stay *here*. Something better is waiting for you *there*."

In other words, "here" is the disappointment, the bad medical report, the dream that didn't work out. If you stay "here," you'll be discouraged. You have to go "there." Sometimes the reason God doesn't comfort us in the "here," in the disappointment, is because He doesn't want us to stay where we are. Yes, the loss is painful. Yes, the setback wasn't fair, but God is not "here." He's gone ahead. He's waiting for you "there." God is not in your past, in what you lost, in what didn't work out. He's in your future. Don't get stuck in "here." Move forward into "there." "There" is where the vindication is, where new beginnings are, where you'll find your healing. If these three ladies had stayed at the tomb in self-pity, saying, "We can't believe this happened," they would never have seen the "there." They would never have seen the Lord.

Are you living in the "here," while God is waiting for you "there"? Are you stuck in a disappointment, bitter over a bad break, angry over what didn't work out? It's time to leave "here" and go "there." "There" is where God is waiting for you. "There" is where the blessing is. The disappointment is simply a season. It's not the rest of your life. God has already gone ahead. God has already lined up the next chapter. Your house was damaged in the storm. That's "here." Yes, that's disappointing. The good news is, God has gone ahead. He's waiting for you "there." He has restoration already lined up.

My father had been pastoring a church for many years, and he was very successful. They had just built a beautiful new sanctuary. Then my sister Lisa was born with something like cerebral palsy, and my dad began to search the Scriptures in a new way. He found how God is a healer and how Jesus came that we might live an abundant, victorious life. He started sharing this good news with his congregation, but it didn't fit in their church's denominational teaching. People whom he had known for years suddenly turned on him. My father ended up having to leave that church. He was so disappointed. He never dreamed he'd have to start all over. His "here" wasn't fair, but what he couldn't see was that God had already lined up Lakewood and was waiting for him "there." If my father had stayed in the "here," he would have missed his destiny.

What am I saying? The "here" is not the end. The disappointment, the loss, and the betrayal are temporary. God has already gone ahead. Don't let bitterness hold you back. Don't sit around in self-pity. Move forward into "there." "There" is where God will pay you back. "There" is where He'll do more than you can ask or think of.

Consider This

Naomi was so discouraged she didn't think she could go on. She even changed her name from Naomi, which means "my joy," to Mara, which means "bitter." She said, "Call me Mara, because the Almighty has made my life very bitter. I went away full, but the LORD has brought me back empty" (Ruth 1:20–21). Have you ever gone out full, with big dreams and big goals, but things didn't work out the way you had planned? Describe your experience and how you responded.

....
....
....
....
....
....
....
....
....
....
....
....
....
....
....
....

What the Scriptures Say

But one thing I do: Forgetting what is behind and straining toward what is ahead, I press on toward the goal to win the prize for which God has called me heavenward in Christ Jesus.

Philippians 3:13–14

Then Deborah said to Barak, "Go! This is the day the LORD has given Sisera into your hands. Has not the LORD gone ahead of you?"

Judges 4:14

Thoughts for Today

Words can never adequately convey the incredible impact of our attitude toward life. The longer I live the more convinced I become that life is ten percent what happens to us and ninety percent how we respond to it.

Charles Swindoll

Every experience God gives us, every person He puts in our lives, is the perfect preparation for the future that only He can see.

Corrie ten Boom

Why believe the devil instead of believing God? Rise up and realize the truth about yourself—that all the past has gone, and you are one with Christ, and all your sins have been blotted out once and forever. O let us remember that it is sin to doubt God's Word. It is sin to allow the past, which God has dealt with, to rob us of our joy and our usefulness in the present and in the future.

Martyn Lloyd-Jones

....
....
....
....
....
....
....
....
....
....
....

A Prayer for Today

Father in heaven, thank You that You're not in the past, in what I lost, in what didn't work out, in the disappointments and the setbacks. Thank You that You've gone ahead and You're lining up the next great chapter of my life. Help me to not get stuck in the "here" when You want me to move forward into the "there" and a future that is more than I can ask or think of. I believe that You're going to bring me into a new sense of freedom, better relationships, greater joy, and cause me to rise higher. In Jesus' Name. Amen.

Takeaway Truth

Today is a gift. We have no guarantee that we're going to be here tomorrow. Time is too short to live offended and bitter, in self-pity. Don't let negative things from your past cause you to be sour and sit on the sidelines of life. God knows what you didn't get. Quit trying to get people to pay you back; go to God, and He'll make it up to you. Start dreaming again. Start loving again. Start believing again.

NEXT LEVEL
THINKING

Remove the Shame

CHAPTER NINETEEN

Shame Off You

›› *Key Truth* ‹‹

Shame is one of the enemy's favorite tools. He is called "the accuser," and he will remind you of every mistake and every failure you've ever made, even about things that weren't your fault. But the Scripture speaks of how God has removed our shame. When the enemy says, "Shame on you," God says, "Shame off you. I've forgiven and redeemed you."

tarting in our childhoods, we've all heard the phrase "Shame on you." When you didn't clean your room or were mean to your little brother or sister, it was, "Shame on you." As adults, the words still play in our thoughts. If you fell back into a bad habit, you told yourself, "Shame on you." If you went through a divorce, the message was repeated over and over: "Shame on you." We don't realize how destructive shame is. We use it to try to convince people to do better, but shame only causes us to feel guilty and unworthy.

A young lady told me that when she was a teenager she had a baby whom she wasn't able to keep, so she put the baby up for adoption. Now ten years later she said, "I feel so ashamed for abandoning my baby. I can't sleep at night thinking about what a terrible mother I am." The enemy is constantly whispering to her, "Shame on you." But the Scripture speaks of how God has removed our shame. Whether it was your fault or somebody else's fault, you don't have to carry the heavy load of guilt, or beat yourself up over past mistakes, or feel wrong on the inside. When the enemy says, "Shame on you," God says, "Shame off you. I've forgiven you. I've redeemed you."

The young lady asked me, "Do you think God will forgive me?" I said, "I know God will forgive you. The question is, Will you forgive yourself and shake off the shame?" I have found that it is more difficult to forgive ourselves than it is to forgive other people. That's why the enemy works overtime to try to bring guilt and shame on you, to make you feel as though you don't deserve to be blessed. You have to turn off the accusing voices. You may have made mistakes, but the moment you asked God to forgive you, He not only forgave you but He took it one step further and doesn't even remember it anymore.

During the hundreds of years when the Israelites were slaves in Egypt, they were very beaten down, not only physically but emotionally. They were constantly told that they were no good, that they couldn't do anything right, and that they deserved to be punished. Over time the Israelites let that steal their sense of value. They felt inferior and insecure, ashamed of who they were. But after 430 years of enduring it, God brought them out of slavery, out of the abuse. As they were approaching the Promised Land, God said to them, "Today I have rolled away the reproach of Egypt from you" (Josh. 5:9). The word *reproach* means "shame, blame, disgrace." They couldn't go into the Promised Land with the shame of feeling unworthy and not valuable. God had to roll the reproach off them.

In the same way, before you can reach your highest potential, you have to get rid of any shame. You may have made mistakes and other people may have done you wrong. But you can't sit around feeling guilty and condemned, blaming yourself and blaming others. Whatever your Egypt is—a divorce, or an addiction, or somebody who did you wrong—God is saying, "This day—not tomorrow, not next week, not six months from now but today—I am rolling away the reproach, the guilt and the shame." Now it's up to you to accept it. When you get up in the morning and you hear that voice saying, "Shame on you," answer right back, "No, shame off me! My reproach has been taken away."

Consider This

Before you can reach your highest potential, you have to get rid of any shame. What is your Egypt, so to speak, and what is God saying to you about it?

....
....
....
....
....
....
....
....
....
....
....
....
....
....
....
....
....
....
....
....
....

What the Scriptures Say

"I, even I, am he who blots out your transgressions, for my sake, and remembers your sins no more."

Isaiah 43:25

As Scripture says, "Anyone who believes in him will never be put to shame."

Romans 10:11

....
....
....
....
....
....
....
....
....
....
....
....
....
....
....
....
....
....

Thoughts for Today

The law screams, "Shame on you!" Grace screams, "Shame off you!"

John Gray

If you think you've blown God's plan for your life, rest in this. You, my beautiful friend, are not that powerful.

Lisa Bevere

Bring your sins, and He will bear them away into the wilderness of forgetfulness, and you will never see them again.

Dwight Moody

A Prayer for Today

Father in heaven, thank You that I don't have to carry the heavy load of guilt, or beat myself up over past mistakes, or feel wrong on the inside because You have removed my shame. Thank You that I have the power to turn off the accusing voices about past mistakes because You forgave my sin the moment I asked You to, and You don't even remember it anymore. I believe that You have rolled away the reproach, that I have been approved and accepted by You, and I declare, "Shame off me!" In Jesus' Name. Amen.

....
....
....
....
....
....
....
....
....
....
....
....
....
....
....
....
....

Takeaway Truth

You may have failed in some area of your life. That's what you did, that's not who you are. You may have had some bad breaks. That's what happened to you; that is not your identity. When thoughts of guilt and shame try to label you, you have to remind yourself, "I am not who people say I am or who circumstances say I am. I am who God says I am. He says I am approved, I am accepted, I am valuable, and I am a masterpiece."

CHAPTER TWENTY

Healing Begins When We Get Honest

» *Key Truth* «

If you're still struggling in an area today, there is no shame in asking for help. Sometimes we think we're supposed to be perfect, so we can't let anybody know we have a bad habit, an addiction, or a struggle. We would be embarrassed if others knew. Don't let shame keep you isolated. Real healing begins when we get honest.

t's easy to hide things in our lives and let people see only what we want them to see. We would be embarrassed if others knew about our struggle. We let shame keep us isolated. But healing only begins when we get honest. The Scripture says, "Admit your faults to one another and pray for each other so that you may be healed" (James 5:16 TLB). There are some things that you can't overcome on your own. You need somebody to stand in faith with you. I'm not saying you have to announce your struggle to others, but you can find a person of integrity whom you can trust to walk with you through it. There's something about getting it out in the open. Don't let the fear of what other people think keep you from your miracle. Everybody is dealing with something. The people who always look fine on the outside, they're good at pretending.

Even in the Scripture, all the heroes of faith had their weaknesses. One day Peter was cursing people out, denying that he knew Jesus. Weeks later he was telling a crippled man to rise and walk and preaching to thousands. One day David was defeating a giant, and on another day he was committing adultery and having the lady's husband killed. He tried to hide it for a year. Finally David was confronted by the prophet Nathan, and he got it out in the open, confessed his faults, and God restored him. One day Noah was saving his family from the Flood. On another day he was drunk on the floor of his tent.

Many times the things you're struggling with didn't start with you. They were passed down. Now this is your opportunity to put an end to it. You can be the one to break the negative cycle in your family. The first step is to shake off the shame. Don't be embarrassed. Don't try to hide it. You don't have to go through life pretending. If you'll be honest, go to God and ask Him for help, find a friend to walk it out with you, then you can overcome anything that's holding you back. The forces for you are greater than the forces against you.

I received a letter from a teenage girl who told how she struggled with anorexia. On top of that, she was cutting herself. That seemed to be the only way she could find relief from the pain she felt on the inside. She came from a well-respected family and was too embarrassed to tell anyone. She felt ashamed of who she was, and she was overwhelmed with guilt for injuring herself. She knew it was wrong, but she kept hearing the voices say, "You're not valuable. You're no good. Look at you and what you've done to yourself." One day she heard me talking about how God will heal your hurts, how He'll give you beauty for ashes, and how there's no shame in being honest and going to God and asking for help. That day she made the decision that she wasn't going to pretend anymore. She told her parents what was going on. They got her the help she needed. Today she's not only healthy, whole, and free, but she's a counselor who is helping other young people who are struggling with the same issues.

That's what happens when you shake off the shame. God will take your scars and turn them into stars. He'll use you to help others.

Consider This

Everyone has issues. What powerful principle was reflected in the teenage girl who struggled with anorexia that will help you confront any issues of shame?

....

....

....

....

....

....

....

....

....

....

....

....

....

....

....

....

....

....

....

....

What the Scriptures Say

"Do not be afraid; you will not be put to shame. Do not fear disgrace; you will not be humiliated. You will forget the shame of your youth and remember no more the reproach…"

Isaiah 54:4

…you will be called by a new name that the mouth of the LORD will bestow. You will be a crown of splendor in the LORD's hand, a royal diadem in the hand of your God.

Isaiah 62:2–3

Thoughts for Today

I have learned that breaking free from the shackles of shame is not an overnight experience or a quick-fix, ten-step process. It is, however, a grand, ongoing adventure of discovering the depths of God's love and the huge scope of God's power to transform us, re-create us, and continually renew us.

Christine Caine

Shame's healing encompasses the counterintuitive act of turning toward what we are most terrified of. We fear the shame that we will feel when we speak of that very shame…. But it is in the movement toward another, toward connection with someone who is safe, that we come to know life and freedom from this prison.

Curt Thompson

Your focus should be on following Christ, not looking over your shoulder and regretting what you can't change. Shame is a prison, but the door to your cell is open. Jesus calls you to follow Him in the freedom of grace.

Brian Houston

....

....

....

....

....

....

....

....

....

A Prayer for Today

Father in heaven, thank You that I don't have to live a life of
pretending that I have it all together and hiding things from
others. I come to You with my issues and faults and ask You to
help. I ask You to help me find a friend whom I can trust to walk
it out with me. Thank You that I can shake off the shame and
guilt, knowing that You will heal my hurts and give me beauty
for ashes. I believe and declare that not only will I forget
the shame of the past but that You are going to pay me
back double. In Jesus' Name. Amen.

Takeaway Truth

The next time you hear that voice whispering,
"Shame on you," instead of believing that lie,
beating yourself up, and getting depressed,
rise up and declare, "No, shame off me!"
Nothing that was done to you, and nothing
that you have done, has changed your identity.
You are still a child of the Most High God.
If you'll start shaking off the guilt and the shame,
you'll see the healing, the breakthrough,
and the new levels.